Stop Paddling/ Start Sailing

A journey and some ideas

Roger Smith

PublishAmerica
Baltimore

First printing

ISBN: 1-4137-2020-X
PUBLISHED BY PUBLISHAMERICA, LLLP
www.publishamerica.com
Baltimore

Printed in the United States of America

Readers are likely to gain the most from this book by setting a couple of hours aside in a quiet place and reading it in one go from cover to cover. It is deliberately short enough to be read all in one go.

Throughout this book bi-polar disorder may be referred to as Manic Depression or MD which are common terms in the UK.

"I finally managed to find time to read your book! It is fascinating to me to see the ideas of memetics being used in such a personal and life-transforming way."

Dr Susan Blackmore, author of *The Meme Machine*

Acknowledgments

Firstly I must thank Mukesh Bhatt for believing I could turn my ideas into a book and then Rosie who read the first draft of just about every page.

Colleagues at worked helped enormously, making the book more acceptable to a wider audience, especially Lucy, Eli, J.T., Jan Ayar and Steve Shardlow.

Thanks go to two nurses, Betty and Paula, who were around when I had been ill and later read and commented as the book neared completion.

Most of the remaining grammatical errors were ironed out by Jean.

Finally, my thanks go to two men I have yet to meet in person who offered advice by e-mail—Tom Riley and John Platts.

Contents

What My Book is About

Writing about Life

"Life is…." How often have we heard a sentence start with these two words? "Life is a minestrone," "Life is a bowl of cherries," "Life is a box of chocolates" and so on. Sentences like this intrigue and may amuse, but they do not seem to say a lot that helps us understand life.

At the other extreme, biographies and autobiographies have been written that try to explain individual lives. They do just that, they tell us about an individual, but only a fraction of the book will be applicable to the reader's life.

Another attempt at describing human life is the textbook that tells us what the author has discovered by a combination of reading and living. For me the trouble with these textbooks is that they are usually too long and it can be difficult to apply this kind of "science" to real life.

An alternative to this is to put experiences and conclusions to date in the form of a short, easy-to-read story and then where appropriate add explanations. I have read several books of this type and found they moved me. My intention is to tell my story in this style by putting my life initially in a fantasy world where unnecessary detail can be left out.

In telling my story I hope to better understand myself *and* have the reader say, "Yes, I see what he means." But as well as these obvious objectives I am also hoping my book will show those waiting to write a book about life that it is not necessarily difficult.

My biggest challenge was not what to put in but in deciding what to leave out to keep it short and to make the important points stand out. In doing this I remembered a story I heard about a lady on a management training course who was asked to write the story of her life in just four short chapters. She wrote something like this:

> Chapter 1: I walked down a road and fell down a hole. It was a deep hole. It hurt. It took a long time to climb out.
> Chapter 2: I walked down a road and fell down a hole. It was a deep hole. It hurt. I recognised the hole. It didn't take so long to climb out.
> Chapter 3: I walked down a road. I saw that same hole. I walked around the hole.
> Chapter 4: I walked down a different road.
> The End

When I first heard that story I was with a group of students and we all were struck by it and said that it was amazing that it is so concise and yet says so much.

What this story shows is that you can say a lot about your life in a very few words. These words will not tell the reader a great deal about your life, but will probably have them asking for more information—like "What sort of hole?" and "What sort of other road?"

What I have done is tell my story three times. Version 1 is my story in a nutshell. You could say a skeleton. Version 2 fills in a bit more detail but will seem a fantasy until explained in Version 3, which by filling in real life events becomes the bulk of the book.

Version 1, the short story, looks similar to the one about holes I mentioned a moment ago. I am grateful that I heard this story of holes; otherwise, I would have had no idea how to compress my life onto one page. I guess any similarity must be because I and that other author have seen our experiences in similar ways.

Version 2 is the same story expanded. It is more colourful than Version 1. Some gaps have been filled in so as to form the whole framework for Version 3.

Version 3 is a lot longer as it explains the other two and contains real events. I would not say it is *the* story of my life, but it is a story based on parts of my life and goes some way to explaining how I now view things based upon my experiences. The people are real, although some names have been changed.

Chapter 1

Version 1

I have been travelling down a huge river in a small boat.

For a long time I drifted, then paddled, then drifted, then paddled and so on.

As I went down the river I collected flags.

Suddenly, I went over a waterfall.

At the bottom of these falls I met a boat builder. He gave me *two* rudders for my boat.

Also here I met a hermit. He told me paddling was no good as the paddles we had did not even reach the water.

I drifted on, not paddling now, but simply relying on the rudders and trying to understand the currents.

Suddenly, I went over another waterfall. At the bottom I met an angel who looked after me for a while. Then a boat repairer was there again. He admitted that the two rudders were not effective. He gave me a different kind of rudder and a flag.

I drifted on until I met a lady in a sailing boat. She explained that the flags I was flying were catching the wind and determining where my canoe was going.

I put up lots of flags to catch the wind. The wind blew me over another waterfall. At the bottom a boat builder equipped me with a new improved rudder, which I was grateful for, but now I knew it was the wind I really needed to understand.

I set off again and started to meet others who were learning to sail and am now continuing to explore the big river.

--------------------------- End of Version 1 ---------------------------

Chapter 2

Version 2

I have been travelling down a huge river in a canoe.

For a long time I drifted, then paddled, then drifted, then paddled and so on.

This river is wide. On one side the water runs fast over rocks. On the other side the water is almost stagnant with mud just below the surface and it is thick with reeds. It is impossible to land on either bank.

As I have travelled down the river I have been collecting flags. These have been given to me by others on the river. The flags are in all colours, patterns, shapes and sizes. Some are just cloth flags which I tend to put in the bottom of my canoe, whilst others come complete with enough of a flagpole to allow me to fly them fixed to the side of my canoe.

On my way I was paddling hard, when a friend, also in a canoe, introduced me to a guru who let me have seven special flags. He told me that if I could fly all seven flags I would get where I was going much more quickly. I tried flying the flags and continued to paddle. It was difficult but I found I was going more quickly.

After a while I noticed my boat was going faster and faster. I tried paddling the other way. I shouted and waved for help. People in other boats waved back and said they had never seen anyone go so fast.

I found myself at the top of a waterfall. A second later I was over the edge and falling fast. It was exciting but most of all it was terrifying. After what seemed like an eternity I hit the foaming water at the bottom and was thrown about one moment under the water, then out gasping for air, then under the water again. When I eventually had my boat upright and the water was less choppy I met a boat builder, well, more of a boat repairer than builder. He was odd as he asked many questions but never answered a question. He later gave me *two* rudders for my boat.

I also met a hermit writing a story in a canoe anchored in a quiet place at the bottom of the falls. He spoke very little but on questioning I discovered that he had been over a great many waterfalls. He also turned out to be an expert on paddles and currents. He explained to me that paddling was no good. He pointed out the paddles we had did not even reach the water.

I drifted on, not paddling now, but simply trying to understand the currents and relying on the first of the rudders I had been given. This rudder worked only to move the boat towards the slow muddy side of the river. I found myself stuck in the mud. I was so stuck all I wanted to do was get out and try wading to the bank. I had given up all hope of travelling down river again.

A boat repairer came by and asked if I was really and truly stuck. I said I was. He did not seem to hear my answer, but after I said I was stuck several times he said, "Now use the other rudder."

I was glad to rid myself of this first rudder and swore I would never use it again. At first the second rudder did nothing. There was no current and my boat seemed to be stuck, but then little by little I started to move out into the open water. But this rudder worked only to move the boat towards the fast flowing side of the river and soon I had crossed halfway, then in no time I was in the white water, then I went over another waterfall. It was exciting, but mostly terrifying.

At the bottom I met an angel who looked after me for a while. The angel had a huge presence. Everyone around him seemed small. Like the hermit I had met before, the angel had spent most of his life going over waterfalls and was well equipped to help those new to this way of life. Then a boat repairer was there again. He admitted that the two rudders were not effective and added that normal rudders do not work on boats that are drifting. He gave me a different kind of rudder and a flag. He said this was standard issue for where I was going.

It was here that I started to notice most boats had flags. Some a bit like mine and some exactly like mine. I drifted slowly along with these people, terrified that at any moment I would be going over another waterfall.

I started talking to others in boats with black and white flags and found the new rudder I had been given was very common for boats with this flag. The rudder ensured the boat went in a straight line at all times.... But it did not take account of bends in the river.

At first the way the river bent put me on the slow muddy side, lost among narrow passages through tall reeds. Then as the river bent the other way I drifted into the middle of the river and although I seemed to make progress for a while the bend in the river forced me over to the white water side.

It was here that I saw a sailing boat. I had seen these before but this was different. I was right alongside the sailing boat and seemed to be going at the same speed. I had never thought of sailing before as I only had a canoe. I asked the lady in the boat about sailing and she explained that was what I was already doing with all the flags I was flying. The flags were catching the wind. The wind had blown me onto the dangerous side of the river. I looked around my canoe. I had loads of flags I had been collecting from the people I had met: some were flying, whilst some were lying around my feet.

I started putting up lots of flags. I was going so quickly with the wind blowing me. It was fantastic. Suddenly everything made sense. It was the wind that had been blowing me around on the river.

My boat raced forward. I was suddenly in a place where I could see for miles, hundreds of miles. I was very high up. Then my canoe capsized. It was not designed for sailing. It of course had no keel to stop it blowing over. A moment later the wind and currents took me over another waterfall. Once again, it was exciting, but once again it was mostly terrifying.

At the bottom this time I met characters, who like the hermit and the angel, could tell me more about waterfalls, but this was not of great importance to me. What I wanted was to learn how to sail as this would be my way of avoiding the waterfalls.

There was a boat repairer there who equipped me with a new improved rudder. But there at the side of river I saw what I really wanted. A sailing boat! I asked the boat repairer if I could take it. He said, "Sure, if that is what you want, but there's no sail. Oh! And don't forget your rudder."

I set off again and started to meet others who were learning to sail. I could see now that every boat had lots of flags and that every boat was being blown around by the wind, but the sailing boats were much more stable than canoes.

I was being pushed along by the wind blowing my many flags. As I travelled I learnt to use my new rudder. The lower part was like the previous one, always trying to keep the boat in a straight line. The upper part, however, I found could be quickly adjusted to turn me left or right and hence help keep me mid-stream.

I also started learning about flags and sails.

I noticed how all the sails, when seen up close, were made out of a lot of flags.

I have started to make a sail of my own for my sailing boat. While I am doing this I am continuing to explore more of the big river with others who fly similar flags. Some of us are sailing, others are relying on currents, whilst some are still paddling. To tell the truth I still paddle when I forget myself and all that I have learnt—it is just human nature I guess.

Some of the things I have learnt on my journey:

- Paddling does not work.
- Rudders only work if there is something powering your boat.
- It was the currents that were taking me towards the rapids, marshes and waterfalls, whilst it was the flags I was flying that caught the wind and put me in real danger.
- Flags catch the wind, so more flags make you go more quickly.
- Sailing is the only sensible way to travel in a sailing boat.

---------------------------- End of Version 2 ----------------------------

Chapter 3

Version 3

"Freedom…oh, freedom. That's just some people talking. We're all prisoners walking through this world all alone." So the words of this Eagles song pounded in my head just as my feet pounded the pavement and the rain pounded on the hood of my cagoule. My timing for catching the coach to the Springfields Atomic Energy site was impeccable, as it had been every weekday for the past three months. Still thinking about this song, I turned off North Road down a path I had found to be a useful shortcut. But moments later I was brought to a dead stop.

The footbridge wasn't there! The handrail was there but the bridge was under fast-flowing muddy water. Perhaps I should not have been so surprised, but there again I was young, even naïve, and it had never occurred to me that such a tiny stream could overnight become a torrent.

I had to turn back and go the road way. This would add three minutes to my journey and mean almost certainly missing the bus unless I was to jog for a while.

As I started jogging, my mind corrupted some words from another Eagles song. "How did it ever get this crazy?" I heard myself saying. I had drifted into this lifestyle. I was in grotty digs, with strange characters I had nothing in common with, in a job I seemed to have by default rather than by choosing and in a town 200 miles from home. I decided things had to change.

That day I contacted Jeff Green, a friend I knew from university. After a drink together we decided we could rent a house. All we needed was to find a third person. Jeff said he knew of someone called Dave who wanted to move to Preston. Jeff had never met Dave but told me that Graham, who worked near me, knew Dave. Graham told me which bus Dave caught within the Springfields site. So the next day I boarded that bus and took a guess that the young man near the front would be him. "Dave Masters, I presume" were my words.

Within a week or so the three of us moved into a terraced house on Elmsley Street just a few yards from the bus stop to Springfields. During the rest of our time together we held noisy parties, played in the local darts team, cooked together, became great friends. When it came time to leave Elmsley Street Dave and I hitchhiked to St. Bees Head in Cumbria and walked the 190 miles across to the North Sea. These were great times for me.

I have told this little part of my life in some detail because it illustrates fairly well what I mean by starting my story with…

I have been travelling down a huge river in a canoe.

For a long time I drifted, then paddled, then drifted, then paddled and so on.

I really believed that I would get into unpleasant situations by kind of drifting, but I would get out of them by making a real effort—paddling.

When I was younger no one told me about mood swings. Like most people I became aware of moods in myself and in others. It was not a subject I spent much time thinking about even though I seemed to have periods of being sadder for longer than most people I knew.

I also sometimes got a good feeling of knowing more about how the world works. I tried to put this feeling into words but never thought to write anything down. At these times I concluded that the key to this feeling was to know one essential thing with certainty and then allow everything else to follow on from that. If you ever get the chance to see the film *City Slickers* watch for the moment when a city slicker asks the old cowboy what is his secret to happiness. The old cowboy replies that there is just one thing you need to know. He follows this by saying the city slicker would have to discover what it was for himself.

This feeling of great inspiration/greater knowledge never lasted long and my overall view of moods was simple; sad was bad and the opposite of sad was happy and that was good. I illustrate moods in my story with sad as the slow flowing side and the happy side as fast flowing.

The idea that one could get too happy had never crossed my mind. The idea that one might crave mere contentment (the centre of the river) and give up or do almost anything to achieve it was also an alien concept for most of my life.

This river is wide. On one side the water runs fast over rocks. On the other side the water is almost stagnant with mud just below the surface and it is thick with reeds. It is impossible to land on either bank.

One thing I feel I have done a lot of in my life is meeting new people. This is usually followed by getting to know them a bit and then usually followed by losing touch. It is a shame but that has so often been the pattern of things. However, what I have found in this process is that so many people have little gems of wisdom they are keen to share. Sometimes we can make no real use of them…for example, a steel worker, in his forties, I came to know quite well when I was doing a summer job as a student. He repeatedly told me, "The world is your oyster, don't get stuck in a rut like I have." I remember the words but I do not think they have had a great effect on me. In my story this idea is a flag without a pole.

On the other hand some words of wisdom continue to affect me. For example: The morning after a very late night, I turned up for work an hour late obviously badly hung-over. The boss said, "You know you should *never* be late twice in one day…." This was followed moments later by, "You're so late getting here. Why not go home early." I found the idea funny, but then also logical as if you are so unwell or disorganised to be late for work, then perhaps you should go home early to sort yourself out. Since this time I have applied this logic to my life many times and found myself saying the same words in the same way to colleagues at least half a dozen times. This is an example of a flag with a pole—an idea with a memory attached that has affected my life.

As I have travelled down the river I have been collecting flags. These have been given to me by others on the river. These flags are in all colours, patterns, shapes and sizes. Some are just cloth flags which I tend to put in the bottom of my canoe, whilst others come complete with enough of a flagpole to allow me to fly them fixed to the side of my canoe.

Years after these examples I was at work feeling neither happy nor sad, just stressed, pressured, tortured, tormented or simply plain overworked. I had a few phrases I had heard, which seemed to describe my efforts. Like, "Running just to stay still," or "Nailing jelly to a tree." I talked this over with an associate called Steve Shardlow. He explained that he had been on a course called "The Seven Habits of Highly Effective People," based on a book by Steven R. Covey. I said this sounded like just what I needed to get me out of the rut I was in.

I read the book. I listened to the tape in the car—about 12 times! I memorised each of the habits and how they all fitted together and how they were going to change my life. I felt I was beginning to develop some of the habits and they were beginning to change my life.

On my way I was paddling hard, when a friend introduced me to a guru who let me have seven special flags. He told me that if I could fly all seven flags I would get where I was going much more quickly. I tried flying the flags and continued to paddle. It was difficult but I found I was going faster.

I am not going to explain the seven habits but I will explain what I gradually discovered. I'll use the first habit as an illustration. Covey's first habit for highly effective people is "BE PROACTIVE." It is short. It is simple. It sounds very American. It needs explaining.

Being proactive according to Covey is believing you can change things. It is the opposite of believing things are pre-determined. So what Covey says, and I believe that he is absolutely right, is that people who believe they can change things will be more effective. That does not necessarily mean they will get rich, be famous, etc., but the probability is those sorts of people (the people who have this "be proactive" habit well developed) will get more of what they want—that is assuming they know what they want.

So that is a bit about the first habit. At first it was great knowing about these habits. They fitted in with what I already knew to be true and I thought that if only I developed the habits life would be better. Perhaps I could avoid that slow side of the river.

About this time of my life I was travelling a great deal on my own to visit our company's suppliers. As I was driving I was thinking about being proactive, but the more I drove and thought about this the more convinced I became that most of the time drivers are anything but proactive.

I spent hours in slow moving traffic, where there is no choice but to follow the car in front at the same speed. Even when the road was clear I was governed by my appointment times weighed up against the speed limits and just how safely I could drive. Even exactly where I was on the road was governed by bends and white lines. Overtaking? Here a lot of drivers will differ from what I found. I never really felt I chose to overtake. I just found myself in a position where overtaking was the only sensible option considering safety and the need to get a move on.

So if life were like a journey, then where was the proactivity in life? Were we not always in a queue of traffic on a narrow road with everything determined by what was around us?

I was also starting to question the usefulness of the other habits.

I wanted to go on the Covey course and see if the habits could be made even clearer to me. However, the training officer at work said I knew all I needed to about the habits and all I needed now was to learn how to put them into practice. He sent me on an amazing nine-day management training course simply called "The Human Side of Management."

The course was held close to Sherwood Forest. I was one of about 12 trainees. We were paired off for the week and called "managers." It was our job to lead teams of young people through all sorts of games and generally look after them for the following week. A typical team was made up of the two managers, one veteran (been on the course before), one disabled person (our team had a lady aged about 22 in a wheelchair) and several children aged about 12 to 16. The other people at the school also joined teams, so for example we had the social worker in our team.

Right from the beginning I found the course hard. The hours were long. I could not understand how the course fitted in with my job where I never dealt with the disabled or kids. I was, however, determined to do my best and most of all I was determined to get to the end of the week. The first night I slept less than four hours. The next night there was a tutorial that went on past midnight, I had a strong cup of coffee just before it ended. *I slept zero hours!* The next night I was on duty in helping ensure all the young people were in bed by about midnight when I came across a youngster complaining of severe stomach pains and stayed up with him and the nurse. When I went back to my room I couldn't sleep again. The next day I stopped drinking coffee. The next night I could not sleep again. My mind was going faster and faster. It would not switch off.

I had no sensible words to describe what was happening to me. All I could say was that I was going mad. I continued to tell myself that at some point I would surely be so tired I would sleep, but it just didn't happen. I decided to tell the social worker I was "going mad." I explained about not sleeping. She said, "Roger, you're fine."

So far as she could see I was performing well on the course. I knew I looked fine, but I knew I was not fine in my head. There were only a few days to go and that night we were due to have our first free evening since starting, so I decided to go straight to bed as the day's exercises finished.

As I lay there in the broad daylight of the hot July evening I heard voices talking about going into town. I could not sleep and thought what an opportunity it was to go out with the real managers (I never viewed myself as one of them as at work I had no-one to manage). As the evening went on my lack of sleep very much got the better of me. Everything was becoming surreal.

Back in my room I couldn't sleep. Suddenly it dawned on me—it was the room that was the problem. It smelt! It seemed to be above a boiler room or something and there was a constant hum. It was always hot. I remembered the nurse had been offered the room and refused it and I had been put in there as no one else wanted that room. At 2am I moved to an empty room at the far end of the corridor.

After a while I noticed my boat was going faster and faster. I tried paddling the other way. I shouted and waved for help. People in other boats waved back and said they had never seen anyone go so fast.

The beer knocked me out and I slept until the sun streamed through the window. But it was too little sleep too late. The world continued to be strange. I started to be strange. I told some kids I was from Mars, which was not totally untrue as that was the company I worked for—Mars Inc. That day our team started to fall apart and sometime in the afternoon the head of the people running the course met with my fellow manager and me and asked what was wrong. My colleague was speechless. He just seemed to freeze. I don't think he had particularly seen anything wrong with the way things were going. He had no answers. The head man turned his attention on me. I did not choose to get up and leave the room—it just happened. I found I had no control over myself.

I found myself at the top of a waterfall. A second later I was over the edge and falling fast. It was exciting but most of all it was terrifying.

From that room I ran and ran, it was as if I were a kid again. I was barefoot but I simply ran into the forest and disappeared from the world. I had unlimited energy. I picked up a discarded steering wheel and used it to cut branches off dead trees. I had so much energy and I was so angry because *he* had forced me to break one of the course rules. That was not to leave the training centre grounds. What I was thinking now was no longer rational. I believed they might send the police after me. For a while I hid, lying in the undergrowth. I felt like Robin Hood. I felt like David Bowie in the film *The Man Who Fell to Earth*. I ran again. I knew things would never be the same again. I felt I would be locked up if caught. How would my family cope now that I was mad?

I did other crazy things over the next few hours, like standing in a full water trough and shouting at the top of my voice, "God, I'm lost." I still felt angry. I also felt frightened…but of nothing in particular. Then I felt incredibly lonely as I knew for certain no one could ever understand why I was suddenly so different. I travelled on and on until eventually running up a grassy hill I cut my foot.

It was a big cut and I looked around to see how this had happened. I couldn't see anything, but the blood convinced me I must turn around and seek sanctuary in the first aid room. The nurse would understand.

Well, my foot was never treated but while I was talking to the nurse the head man came in the room. I threatened to hit him if he did not leave me alone. I saw it as his fault that the rules of the course were so impossible and that no one helped me before I snapped. He left and called a doctor who recommended I spend some time in a psychiatric unit.

After what seemed like an eternity I hit the foaming water at the bottom and was thrown about one moment under the water, then out gasping for air, then under the water again.

There followed quite a few days of very scary times. Firstly I was in small unit attached to a general hospital, then home, where I failed to take my medication, then onto a large very old institution that was due to be closed down. For a while I became a little better and then became much worse. Eventually after an injection I slept for about 16 hours. Very gradually, over several weeks, my world returned to something like normal, but there again it was never to be the same.

A heath professional at the hospital told me that the mania from which I was suffering was due entirely to a chemical imbalance that in turn affected my thinking. I was later to think a lot about this idea that what we think is determined by chemistry.

It was at this time that I met the man who was to be my consultant and torturer.

When I eventually had my boat upright again and the water was less choppy I met a boat builder, well, more of a boat repairer than builder. He was odd as he asked many questions but never answered a question. He later gave me two rudders for my boat.

The first of what I am now calling rudders was Haloperidol. To me in my confused state this was Halo Peril Medicine, which was clearly something prescribed to people with fear of heaven. If this was not the meaning of the name why did they give it such a name? I still could not sleep so they offered me a tablet called "Zimmerframe," which I said I didn't like the sound of. I was no less troubled when they told me its other name was "Soppy Clone." The Haloperidol had terrible side effects for me. It didn't take long for me to become depressed. In fact I became more depressed than I had ever been. It was a struggle for me to do anything.

(Much later I found this drug was really called Zopiclone, also known as Zimovane.)

A new man came onto the ward. He kept to himself, either sleeping or writing. I approached him and learnt that he suffered from schizophrenia and had had many manic episodes. He was quiet and didn't try to push his views, but I was intrigued by his writings even though at the time I could read no more than one sentence at a sitting and even then probably not make any sense of it.

One afternoon we went for a walk in the hospital grounds, and I told him that despite all that had happened I still believed we were in control of our destinies. He then told me some of the things that had happened to him and how those things had convinced him that everything was pre-determined. He also talked to me about physics (he had a degree in physics), of which I already understood sufficient to know that everything that happens is influenced by what happened a moment before. The way he explained these things changed my thinking forever....

After our walk I was tired, but my new friend said he would stay outside a little longer. I climbed the stairs back to the ward, and as I did so my tiredness and the effects of the drugs made me struggle over each step. With each step I said to myself, "I am *determined* to get to the top." But with alternating steps I found myself saying the same words but with different meanings. For one step I meant determined as in "my willpower will get me to the top" and for the next step I meant determined as in "pre-determined." I was so tired I did not know if I would get to the top in one go or do what I had on a previous occasion and sit down half way up.

I thought about this stair climbing a lot over the coming weeks and months as this was the moment I first admitted to myself that I was not in control in the way I had previously thought. In fact I was now admitting that I might really have no control at all over events.

Some other time, I had read a little about determinism and found it can be put into categories. Three commonly used categories are:

1. Genetic determinism—it was determined before we were born.
2. Psychic determinism—it was determined by what happened to us as we grew up.

3. Environmental determinism—it is determined by what is going on around us now.

I could see all three were true for me but there was still something missing. I continued to look for what was missing in conversation and in reading anything I thought might help.

I drifted on, not paddling now, but simply trying to understand the currents and relying on the first of the rudders I had been given. This rudder only worked to move the boat towards the slow muddy side of the river. I found myself stuck in the mud. I was so stuck all I wanted to do was get out and try wading to the bank. I had given up all hope of travelling down river again.

As I said the first rudder was Haloperidol. Taking it resulted in me being suicidal. In a short while I had become a wreck. It was only when my consultant saw me crying and heard me say I was very sad indeed that he finally gave me alternative drugs.

The boat repairer asked if I was really and truly stuck. He did not seem to hear my answer, but after I said I was stuck several times he said, "Now use the other rudder."

After trying Amitryptilene, he gave me Prozac.

I was glad to rid myself of this first rudder and swore I would never use it again. At first the second rudder did nothing. There was no current and my boat seemed to be stuck, but then little by little I started to move out into the open water. But this rudder only worked to move the boat towards the fast flowing side of the river and in no time I had crossed halfway, then in no time I was in the white water, then I went over another waterfall. It was exciting, but mostly terrifying.

I do not need to describe in detail this second manic episode. I need only to say it was every bit as bizarre and frightening as the previous one. In the four months since I was released from the old psychiatric unit it had been closed down and a new state-of-the-art unit opened.

On arriving I was desperately thirsty. But it was the same old staff. "No drink until tea time," I was told.

At the bottom I met an angel who looked after me for a while. The angel had a huge presence. Everyone around him seemed small. Like the hermit I had met before the angel had spent most of his life going over waterfalls and was well equipped to help those new to this way of life.

Angel? Well, he was no angel. He was well over six foot with broad shoulders and wore a black leather jacket. His eyes were the bluest I have ever seen— almost as if they had lights in them. He showed me where I could get really cold water. The nurses disapproved. In fact they seemed to disapprove of everything he did. The angel helped me get back on my feet. I can't say he taught me anything profound. He was just one of many patients who helped one another whilst on the psychiatric ward.

Then a boat repairer was there again. He admitted that the two rudders were not effective and added that normal rudders do not work on boats that are drifting. He gave me a different kind of rudder and curiously a black and white flag. He explained this was standard issue for where I was going.

Clearly the Prozac had done me no favours. It had simply made me high again. Up to then I had not been diagnosed as needing a mood stabiliser. But all of a sudden it was decided this was what I needed and I was diagnosed as suffering from bi-polar disorder which in the UK is widely known as manic depression (MD).

To some people such a diagnosis could be a real blow, but to me at that time it was such a relief. At last they knew what was wrong with me. At last I could read about my illness and begin to understand it. At last I could look into what might make me better. I have described the diagnosis as a flag on my boat. Not the only flag, just another one.

The different rudder was lithium. I hated having to take it. I put on two stone in weight in about two weeks. "That's not possible!" I am sure some people will say, but believe me, this is the sort of effect some psychiatric drugs can have.

It was here that I noticed most people had at least one flag a bit like mine and some exactly like my mine. I drifted slowly along with these people, terrified that at any moment I would be going over another waterfall.

In hospital I met others who also suffered mood swings. I found out about the Manic Depression Fellowship. I went along to some meetings at their nearest group, 20 miles away, and realised I was far from alone, but that those owning up to having MD were well spread out.

I recovered enough to go back to work. It was not easy as I was generally depressed, finding the lithium stabilised my mood at somewhere just below contented. More like very sad.

I remember the next winter very well. I would drive to and from work not really caring if I completed the journeys. On the dark homeward journeys I continued to think about the idea of things being determined for us rather than being determined by us. I had been reading articles about brain chemistry and chemistry of the senses. Knowing that my moods were now controlled by a drug I was interested in these topics. As I drove I thought up the following poem. It is not necessarily about people on drugs—it is about everyone. It is not much of a poem as I am no poet, but it went something like this:

We all think. We are thinking.
We all *think* we are thinking,
But it's only chemistry.

We all feel. We are feeling.
We all *think* we are feeling,
But it's only chemistry.

We all see. We are seeing.
We all *think* we are seeing,
But it's only chemistry.

We all hear. We are hearing.
We all *think* we are hearing,
But it's only chemistry.

We all believe. We are believing.
We all *think*, we are thinking,
But it's only chemistry.

It is pretty gloomy stuff, but it was a gloomy time for me. I had accepted that I was not in control of things, but that there was something missing. I understood that physics and chemistry work pretty much like snooker balls. Once a ball is hit the outcome may not be predictable, but it is predetermined. I understood that what goes on in the head is just some rather complex and apparently fast chemistry. But if this was all there was to life then why did so few people see it that way? There seemed to be some missing science, beyond chemistry, physics and biology. Philosophy interested me but it was not the thing that was missing. I knew what this thing was not, but I had no idea what it was or if I would ever find it.

The new rudder I had turned out to be very common for boats with this black and white flag. The rudder ensured the boat went in a straight line at all times…. But it did not take account of bends in the river!

Having met more people with MD I found quite a few were on lithium. I also found lithium only seemed to work if everything in your life was pretty stable. But life's not always like that. Things change. There are bends in the river.

At first the way the river bent put me on the slow muddy side, lost among narrow passages through tall reeds. Then as the river bent the other way I drifted into the middle of the river and although I seemed to make progress for a while the bend in the river forced me over to the white water side.

As I got back to work full time and as my responsibilities at work increased, so did the usual pressures that "normal" people cope with so easily. I was not coping so well. Things were getting difficult again. I needed something to bring me back to the middle of the river but lithium was not going to do that.

It was here that I saw a sailing boat. I had seen these before but this was different. I was right alongside the sailing boat and seemed to be going at the same speed. I had never thought of sailing before as I only had a canoe. I asked the lady in the boat about sailing and she explained, that was what I was already doing with all the flags I was flying. The flags were catching the wind. The wind had blown me onto the dangerous side of the river. I looked around my canoe. I had loads of flags I had been collecting from the people I had met, some were flying, whilst some were lying around my feet.

One lunchtime I picked up a copy of *The New Scientist* magazine (dated 13/ 3/99) and was instantly struck by some words on the front page referring to an article in that edition. Could this be the missing piece of my jigsaw?

I read the article and could hardly believe what I was reading. At last someone did seem to be trying to answer my question of "Why if everything is pre-determined do so few people see that to be the case?" The theory that was briefly described also explained so much about human evolution and behaviour.

The article was written by Dr Susan Blackmore, a senior lecturer in psychology. I wrote to her saying how impressed I was with the way she explained things and asking for her opinion as to whether her ideas might help those with mental health issues.

The theory put forward by Dr Blackmore was to do with memes (pronounce meems). I had never heard of such things. I had never used the word, meme. But now I discovered memes were everywhere and for me made sense of everything.

I tried to explain memes to several people, with very little success, finding no one I met felt they needed the idea. They had gone through all their lives without even knowing the word. Meme theory (memetics) was not taught at school. It was not talked about in the pub. So, why should they want to know?

I wanted to explain what I had found, but had no one to tell and lacked the words to tell it. The following is something I wrote at the time. It looks at one aspect of memetics, in that memes are constantly competing for brain space, bombarding our consciousness every waking minute. I had been thinking of memes as being like Lego pieces (toy building bricks) that were constantly thrown at us, but felt this concept was too crazy, so I imagined each meme being a raindrop or a type of rain. Here is the story exactly as I wrote it. It could easily be called "*Memes* like rain." I was pretty manic when I wrote it, so it needs careful attention as I believe it says far more than I could ever put in so few words whilst in a non-manic state.

* * *

Imagine: Ideas Like Rain

A colourful analogy by Roger Smith

Imagine a land, a wonderful land, where it rains in colour. There are scarlet showers and pink plops. Sometimes there is purple rain mixed with the blues. In this land it rains every day, so rain is seen as neither good nor bad.

From the mountains, streams each of a different colour-mix tumble over iridescent waterfalls. A myriad of waterwheels turn like kaleidoscopes, but barely mix the multicoloured droplets. The colours mix a little more in the wide meandering rivers before discharging into the deep brown lakes.

Every morning scattered showers start early, with heavier rain during the day. Although some regions stay dry it is always raining somewhere during the daylight hours.

But in this strange land the night is just about the opposite. As the sun goes down the clouds blow away and a pleasant breeze dries the puddles.

Water is collected from puddles, ponds, lakes and rivers. It is compared with existing stocks before being stored. Although most colours have been seen before, new hues are discovered every day. Further new hues for export are produced by mixing stored waters.

Umbrellas are fixed above ornamental ponds to keep perfect colour schemes safe from rain of a different colour. Bigger and bigger umbrellas and dams have been built to protect beauty spots such as the tranquil blue lagoon. Work is underway to divert the bloody river which always wreaks havoc after a storm in the mountains.

The land of coloured rain is mostly a pleasant place, but there are two dramatic weather phenomena. These are the rainbow deluge and the ice cube hail storms.

Rainbow deluge occurs when a whirlwind whisks water from many ponds at the same time. This leads to huge drops of unmixed colours falling at a devastating rate washing away all in the path of the multicoloured flood waters.

The ice cube hail follows periods of exceptionally cold weather. The strangely uncoloured slow melting cubes block the rivers bringing everything to a halt.

Both phenomena lead to "wishy-washying" of all unprotected water and eventually to flooding around the deep brown lakes. Tints only return to normal after a long period of warm showery weather.

Roger Smith   5/4/1999

* * *

I started putting up lots of flags. I was going so fast with the wind blowing me. It was fantastic. Suddenly everything made sense. It was the wind that had been blowing me around on the river.

This describes the days between finding out about memes and my next manic episode.

My boat raced forward. I was suddenly in a place where I could see for miles; hundreds of miles. I was very high up. Then my canoe capsized. It was not designed for sailing. It of course had no keel to stop it blowing over. A moment later the wind and currents took me over another waterfall! Once again, it was exciting, but once again it was mostly terrifying.

"*I have found, the world is round*" are some simple words from a Bee Gees song, but this described so well how I felt about memes at that time and to some extent still feel to this day. I did not feel I had been told something but I had *found* it out. What I had *found* seemed of huge significance, but perhaps as with some of the early people who realised that the *world is round* it mattered little to the folks around them. No amount of writing or talking was going to allow me to tell others what I had found. Why should people in canoes want to know about sailing?—it would seem to them to be a dangerous thing for any canoeist to be investigating.

I was back on the psychiatric ward when the reply arrived from Susan Blackmore. It was polite and encouraging but realistic, in that she said she had no experience of MD.

Just before going into hospital I had bought Susan Blackmore's book *The Meme Machine*. As soon as I was able to read again I read the book and started to think how I could make use of this knowledge.

At the bottom this time I met characters, who like the hermit and the angel, could tell me more about waterfalls, but this was not a of great importance to me. What I wanted was to learn how to sail as this would be my way of avoiding the waterfalls.

Two of the people I met were a husband and wife. She had gone manic (again) and he, unable to cope, with secret service men, aliens, etc., had attempted suicide. Now in a calmer mood I talked with each of them (they were on separate wards) and as I did so thought more and more about how memes could be said to be controlling all our lives. I wanted to learn more about memetics and somehow be able to share what I was learning.

There was a boat repairer there who equipped me with a new improved rudder. But there at the side of the river I saw what I really wanted. A sailing boat! I asked the boat repairer if I could take it. He said, "Sure, if that is what you want, but there's no sail. Oh! And don't forget your rudder."

It was also now clearer than ever that no amount of knowing how the mind works would be likely to guarantee I could stay out of hospital. So I was grateful that my consultant gave me a new drug, Olanzapine, in addition to the lithium. I put on another stone in weight and at first I hated it, but after a few months I made a breakthrough. I started taking the tablets only as I needed them rather than exactly as prescribed. I had managed to understand my moods such that I could take two tablets if I was a bit high, one tablet if about normal and no tablets if I was a bit low. The effect was amazing. Since this time I have been pretty well okay—not being anywhere near having to go to the psychiatric ward.

Was it the drugs that made the difference? They certainly played a part, but if it were that simple wouldn't everyone with MD be cured by now? I knew my success was due both to the drugs and at least equally to a better understanding of my own thinking processes.

As my mental health gradually improved I took a keen interest in the activities of the Manic Depression Fellowship. I went on one of their Self-Management Training Programmes. I believe this was very effective for me as I have not been significantly manic or depressed since. The course gave me a sort of tool kit that allows me to fix myself (my boat if you like) before problems become too severe. I use the techniques I learnt alongside my belief that balanced chemistry and understanding of thinking processes can lead to greater stability.

Whilst on the course I refined the idea that good mental health depends on both good chemistry (drugs, diet etc) AND on improvements in thinking processes. I presented this to others on the course as "The Miracle Cure" (some lyrics from a Billy Joel song). I did this as I knew that most experts say there is no cure for MD.

I found people enjoyed and understood the chemistry part, when I talked about sugars in the blood and so on. However, for me to stand up and present a whole new way of thinking was just not realistic at that time. I needed to sort myself out a bit more and perhaps have a different way of telling my story.

I need to explain this meme idea, but I know it is a difficult message or set of messages to get across.

A meme can be said to be a unit of culture. It can be an idea, a song, just a word or a whole book, a few musical notes or an overture, a painting, a way of building something, a type of car or type of ice cream. It seems crazy to think that almost anything you can think of can be described as a meme. Yet is it not even crazier to think that most people do not have a word that collectively covers these things?

The thing that all memes have in common is that they can be accurately passed on from one mind to another. Sometimes memes are not at all obvious. I remember someone asking me if I was related to a Smith whom they had met at a Squash club. I said it was true my brother played there. He replied that he knew he was right not because we looked alike but because of a facial expression. This expression was a meme we must both have picked up/ learned during childhood.

So are memes picked up like a virus or are they learned like something precious? It does not matter! This is why in my "Imagine" story I say there is neither good nor bad rain. Please do not start thinking "the memes are infecting my brain."

The brain was *designed* to house memes.

The Meme Machine explains that the human brain did not just evolve to be really really big, then one day people started thinking in words, talking, painting and passing on ways of making things. The truth is that the two evolutionary processes of brain enlargement and numbers of memes happened alongside each other. It is just as true to say the human brain/mind was created by the evolution of memes as it was by biological evolution.

So here we all are with brains that can take in new memes every day. Any of these memes can then be passed onto anyone else's brain to be stored and passed on again.

Now this may require a leap into the unknown. Imagine that you are not choosing what you are reading. Just imagine for a moment that the words on the page determine what you read.... It is just as reasonable to say the memes on the page are *choosing* that you should be their next host as it is for you to claim you are choosing what you read or what phrases you might remember.

Imagine you do not choose what you listen to. When you believe you are listening to someone, is it not mainly the words coming from them that are determining what you hear?

In the imagine story this is just what I am doing in suggesting memes arrive at our brains like rain that we cannot avoid. Is this a depressing thought? Not really, it is just a different way of looking at things. There is no reason to say that we control memes, when the memes may really control us. After all we evolved together and we have all lived our lives alongside them.

(If you have time you may wish to read the imagine story (page 37) again to see if it means any more a second time through.)

In the main story I have considered memes to be the wind: a driving force determining our route. I have also considered memes to be flags. As we go through life we pick up certain ideas that stay in our minds and influence our choices. For example one might remember "Don't put all your eggs in one basket" and this may influence one. Alternatively one may remember "Put all your eggs in one basket and watch that basket." Both are particularly memorable memes, both I might consider to be flags as they could in the future influence the choices we appear to be making.

I set off again and started to meet others who were learning to sail. I could see now that every boat had lots of flags and that every boat was being blown around by the wind, but the sailing boats were so much more stable than canoes.

What I am saying when I talk of sailing is not some whole new way of life, but just an occasional shift in a way of looking at things. The difference I see is that those I say are in sailing boats have the stability to admit that maybe they are meme driven (or whatever phrase they want to use for this phenomenon). This can remove the heavy responsibility of "it all depends on me" (paddling) and can remove the "I can't do anything about it" (drifting). It leaves the "sailor" well aware they are an integral part of what is going on, and although they are not totally responsible, neither are they a bystander. Even in potentially very stressful situations, it is possible to be in the thick of it, whilst knowing that things should go well because you have a big brain evolved to cope with enormous numbers of memes and that is all you need to deal with almost any situation.

I was being pushed along by the wind blowing my many flags. As I travelled I learnt to use my new rudder. The lower part was like the previous one always trying to keep the boat in a straight line. The upper part, however, I found could be quickly adjusted to turn me left or right and hence help keep me mid-stream.

The lower part of the rudder was the lithium mood stabiliser. The upper part was as described above the Olanzapine antipsychotic that I have been able to use as a mild sedative.

I also started learning about flags and sails.

So, what is it like sailing rather than simply paddling or drifting?

An example: On a typical morning, for many years, how did I manage to be at work every day at 8am? It has been difficult for me to explain to myself considering I did not have to be there until 9am and considering how painful I found getting up early. Do I believe it was sheer will power? I am sure it wasn't that—I no longer believe in the paddling theory. Was it a habit? I am sure it was not as I was not out of bed at 06:35 at the weekend. I think there were many factors but I now believe the biggest one to be a meme that moved into my head at an early age. This meme/subconscious idea is simply that "responsible/good" people start work early. Where could this have come from? Well, my father always started work early, in fact for many years he would be the one to unlock the factory gates. Then my mother, as a nurse working shifts, had to be at the hospital in very good time. Perhaps a dull answer, but what does that mean in practice? It means that most days I simply do not even try to resist my "get to work on time meme" but also by knowing about this meme I can feel okay about going in at a more sensible time or even being late from time to time.

Thinking about the meme idea sometimes on the way to work I believe helps to prepare me for the bombardment with memes that I will encounter. At work I am just a machine as far as the work-related memes are concerned. There are all those e-mails to be processed—information from faraway places that passes momentarily though my mind looking for a response.

Perhaps it all sounds weird. I am not recommending everyone should start switching to my way of thinking. I am, however, hoping that more people will realise there is a different way of viewing the world.

I noticed how all the sails, when seen up close, were made out of a lot of flags.

An area that intrigues me is memeplexes. Memes like genes group together if it enhances their chances of reproducing. For this reason we find many memeplexes in society.

In my story I have used the sail to represent memeplexes.

Any mass of information might be described as a memeplex. Knowledge of a sport, a job, a religion, a science, a language—all these could be considered to be groups of memes that are transmitted from person to person more effectively because they are grouped together. Some memeplexes are so well designed/evolved that once they are in the brain they are almost impossible to shift. But there again if you have a boat with an excellent sail why change it? Perhaps all that is needed is a good keel on the boat to keep it stable.

Books could be said to be memeplexes as they contain many ideas all bound together. So I do not deny this book is an attempt at creating a memeplex.

I have taken some ideas I have gathered and put them together in a package I can share with friends.

I have started to make a sail of my own for my sailing boat. While I am doing this I am continuing to explore more of the big river with others who fly similar flags. Some of us are sailing, others are relying on currents, whilst some are still paddling.

I end my story by pointing out that however strong my beliefs are that I am driven by determinism (currents) and memes (winds) for much of the time I still struggle on in the same way as those who have no interest in such ideas.

To tell the truth I still paddle when I forget myself and all that I have learnt—it is just human nature I guess.

Some of the things I have learnt on my journey:

• **Paddling does not work.**
I used to believe that I could really change things by making a big effort. But looking back at even the first part of this story—was it really me making a supreme effort or is it not more likely that events such as the flooded stream made the difference?

• **Rudders only work if there is something powering your boat.**
We all control our moods to some extent with chemicals of some kind. It may just be sugary foods, chocolate, alcohol, nicotine, or it may be more powerful drugs. However, as life is always changing, the idea of controlling mood with a single drug seems doomed to failure. The chemicals we take in have to be appropriate to the circumstances we find ourselves in. So although I have been lucky enough to find a combination of drugs that help me control my mood in response to changes going on around me, I view these as no more than something to modify mood rather than the real driving force behind mood change or mood stability.

• **It was the currents that were taking me towards the rapids, marshes or waterfalls,**
I am not asking that you become a fatalist and say you have no control over anything. What I do ask, is that you re*consider* determinism and hopefully agree that most of *what is happening* in your life *is not your fault*. Doing this removes stress. It takes a big weight off your mind.

• **but it was always the winds that pushed me into real danger whilst others avoided it.**
Up until I found out about memes it was as if I had been looking at two sides of a coin. One side I was in control, whilst on the other it was the deterministic forces. Suddenly I was able to see the edge of the coin and the explanation was there, written on the edge. For me it was not appreciating memes that allowed me to become ill. Understanding this force was at work has been a major factor in staying well.

- ***Flags catch the wind, so more flags make you go more quickly.***
Going back to my description of Covey's seven habits, I said I was flying seven flags. Each of the habits is a typical meme—an idea that both appeals and is easily passed on. It is great to have lots of memes and be using them, but is it really good to be going faster—especially if you're not sure where you are going!

- ***Sailing is the only sensible way to travel in a sailing boat.***
The brain evolved to handle information. All day every day it accepts information. It stores it. It may alter it. It may pass it on to others. Just consider for a minute or so that this is all the mind does. Imagine how simple life is if you consider the brain is no more (and no less) than a meme machine. Perhaps briefly consider consciousness as no more than a waterwheel in my "Imagine" story.

So I am suggesting that everyone might benefit from time to time from forgetting about anything else we might think our brains might be doing and just for a while accept that maybe one's mind is simply a meme processor, that works best only when the flow of memes is just right. Life is then all about getting the right flow of memes for your own mind at any given moment. Put in everyday language—the right flow of ideas and so on. It is as simple as wind in sails. It is sailing.

-------------------------- End of Version 3 --------------------------

Chapter 4

So What?
Another Tool for the Toolbox

It is a few months since I wrote Chapters 1 to 3 and several friends have read these chapters. They all said they liked the story, but some left me with a feeling of "So what?"

Perhaps the title suggests this should be some sort of self-help book and my friends were left wondering how this story and the ideas might help them. So I guess this short chapter is for anyone looking for something extra from this book.

If you have *never*:

- felt you had any problems with mental health and feel you have no risks in this area
- suffered from insomnia due to thoughts going around in your head
- doubted your beliefs, religious or otherwise
- had difficulty understanding why you do things
- had difficulty understanding why other people do things
- wanted to understand why people do things

then I guess this chapter is not for you, as you have no reason to change the way you look at the world.

If you have suffered any of the above then being able to see the world from a different perspective may just change things for the better. Some people call this kind of change of perspective a paradigm shift. It does not happen easily. Perhaps the only reason I was able to make this particular shift was because of the things I had been through and a recognition that I might not live much longer if I did not make this paradigm shift. Most people do not have such an overwhelming need to change, but if there is any advantage at all in changing then surely it is worth considering that there might indeed be a different way of looking at things.

If you have suffered any of the above then you have probably been paddling—not "going with the flow." If people have suggested you relax perhaps all they have been suggesting is that you drift (which would of course be going with the flow) but this isn't easy for anyone who has grown up paddling. By considering the world from the memes' point of view I believe I am able both to relax and yet not feel guilty. To stop paddling without feeling I am simply drifting. It is important, particularly for those who know me, to admit that I am not doing this all the time, but *it is* something that can be done frequently and especially at times of crisis thus controlling the sorts of issues listed above.

I believe that knowing a bit about memes helps me see other people's behaviour in a different light. I believe I have become more understanding and forgiving. To me it now seems clear that behaviours that previously seemed difficult to understand or forgive can simply be considered as controlled by memes without the people realising.

As an exercise next time you see two people having an argument (one might be yourself) try to stand back for a moment and realise that the people involved are not doing the arguing. It is simply that the meme in one person's head wants to occupy the other person's head and vice versa. Realise that neither person chose to have the argument. They might think they did, but they are wrong. Consider that this "collision" of ideas was not caused by people paddling (trying hard) nor was it caused by drifting (a lack of effort), but it was due to the ideas themselves which are beyond the control of the arguers and can even be said to be controlling the arguers.

If you are able to see this in an argument in which you are directly involved then it could help diffuse the situation or at least help you not feel so bad about it.

The other example I will offer by way of advice is about insomnia.

Have you ever wished you had an off switch that you could flick at bedtime that would give you a perfect night's sleep and allow you to automatically switch on 100% refreshed in the morning? Why should anyone wish this if they were in control of their thoughts? The reason is clearly that we are not in control of our thoughts. The memes in our heads are in reality beyond our control and if they decide to play for hours and hours at night then there is very little we can do about it. So where is the advice?

The first thing to do is admit the thoughts going on in your head are simply memes—ideas that have probably originated from someone else and have been stewed up in your mind and are now desperate to be passed onto someone else.

Realise you are not creating these thoughts. The thoughts you are having in the dead of night either already exist as memes or are the result of memes interacting in your mind. You have little control over this process just as the sailor has little control over which direction the wind is going to blow. So having understood what is going on, how do you fix insomnia?

If it is already the middle of the night then you will most likely have to resort to what I call a chemical option. This might be one drop of lavender oil on the pillow, an appropriate drink, a tablet, opening the window or something like that. All these are only moderately effective.

What do you need to do to avoid insomnia in the first place? Realise that memes cause insomnia then control the memes getting into your brain during the day and especially in the evening. Think if any memes can be eliminated by say avoiding certain people. Perhaps eliminate some pressure by passing memes onto others—that is tell someone what is worrying you—write a letter or e-mail. Perhaps discourage people from phoning in the evening as this always introduces new memes. I could give loads of examples, but the first thing is to shift your point of view to admit that memes (the winds) are really in control, only then can you live in harmony with them (sailing). That's how it might work for you if you suffer from insomnia.

So is this paradigm shift life-changing? I do not think it has to be. The ideas about determinism and memes if taken on board could be viewed as just "one more tool for the toolbox." It is an idea that can be used any time as needed.

--------------------------- End of Chapter 4 ---------------------------

Chapter 5

MD and Self-Management

I have talked a lot about memes as this is something I believe can help people get out of a rut and as I realise few people have really come to terms with this idea. I have deliberately said little about self-management as I believe these ideas are most effectively grasped by attending a residential course at which the three elements of the Manic Depression Fellowship's Self-Management Programme (Recognition, Action and Maintenance) can be absorbed alongside other people with similar problems. No book is likely to take the place of such a course. I found that working interactively with others in a group, sharing problems and solutions, was the best way of developing understanding of how to self-manage.

I do, however, want to share one small element of the Manic Depression Fellowship's course which I am now privileged to help facilitate. This is the idea of a mood scale that is used to judge your own mood and to communicate to others how you are feeling. One reason I am keen to mention this is that it can be of interest to those with no history of mental illness as most people have mood swings.

The other reason I am keen to mention this is that for me it clearly communicates what bi-polar disorder / manic depression is about, when neither name really conveys exactly what happens when you have the illness. I have found that manic depression can be wrongly interpreted as someone who is depressed in a "manic" way. That is someone who gets very very depressed. Perhaps worse than this it can be interpreted as someone who is mostly sad and occasionally wields an axe! Such ideas are silly but illustrate how many people do not really understand what manic depression (MD) is about.

In simple terms, someone suffering from manic depression is more likely to spend time at the extremes of the mood scale (see opposite) than people without the illness. Most people not suffering from mania or depression are likely to have a mood range between 4 and 6 on the scale. Knowing this makes the meaning of MD much clearer. It is worth noting that most people diagnosed with MD will also be likely to spend much time around mood level 5 and be able to live normal productive lives.

Coming back to memes again for a moment, this scale is itself a powerful meme, in that it is easily copied, it is simple, the gist of it is easy to remember and it can be used by anyone. If you are not yet convinced about memes, then it is simply an idea that is spreading because it is so useful.

MDF, UK Self-Management Training Programme

MOOD SCALE

10	Total loss of judgment, exorbitant spending, religious delusions and hallucinations.
9	Lost touch with reality, incoherent, no sleep, paranoid and vindictive, reckless behaviour.
8	Inflated self-esteem, rapid thoughts and speech, counter-productive simultaneous tasks.
7	Very productive, everything to excess ('phone calls, smoking writing, tea), charming and talkative.
6	Self-esteem good, optimistic, sociable and articulate, good decisions and get work done.
5	Mood in balance, no symptoms of depression or mania. Life is going well and the outlook is good.
4	Slight withdrawal from social situations, concentration less than usual, slight agitation.
3	Feelings of panic and anxiety, concentration difficult and memory poor, some comfort in routine.
2	Slow thinking, no appetite, need to be alone, sleep excessive or difficult, everything a struggle.
1	Feelings of hopelessness and guilt, thoughts of suicide, little movement, impossible to do anything.
0	Endless suicidal thoughts, no way out, no movement, everything is bleak and it will always be like this.

In making use of the scale you will probably find just a few of the phrases apply to yourself at any one moment and these are likely to be in the same box allowing you to say "I'm at four" or "six" or whatever. It is quite likely phrases in adjacent boxes will apply so you might say "I'm at five and a half." It is also possible that phrases in non-adjacent boxes might apply but even if you have to report your mood as, "Mostly five with a bit of three," it is still an effective way of communicating with anyone else who has seen this scale.

Considering how this meme might fit into my story, it could be a flag I am flying (something to communicate to others) or perhaps part of a self-management "sail" (something to help me on my way).

I stress that this is just one small component of self-management. A better understanding of the course is available from MDF at www.mdf.org.uk. I need to say this as this book (and I suspect no book) is a substitute for attending a properly organised self-management training programme.

--------------------------- End of Chapter 5 ---------------------------

Chapter 6

Why I Wrote This Book

"It's good to talk" is just a phrase off an advert, but it can also be so true!

I went to school with a young man now known as Dr Martin Smith. He is not a relation of mine but is my oldest friend and despite living 100 miles apart and having pursued very different careers we have kept in touch and when we meet up we discuss many topics. He is now a senior social worker and has been involved in several research projects. One of these projects was the study of how some people find the telling of their story following some crisis or even long lasting problem in their lives can help them overcome some of the anguish.

When I told Martin that I had been writing bits about my life and some short stories he showed me some of his research papers and I began to better understand why I was doing this writing. It is said that *the greatest hunger of the human soul is to be understood*. Well, I wanted to both be understood and to understand myself.

But I have found people do not easily understand themselves and the process usually involves telling one's story many times. Sometimes the telling and healing process seems to make little progress as the listener can for whatever reason not offer the right sort of interaction. But at other times a listener will nod, encourage and ask questions at just the right time and the healing process seems to work.

I had told bits of my story to many people, but I simply could not put my message across in anything like the way I needed to. I did not have the words to describe what I had been through. To explain myself I wrote "Imagine" that has become part of this book and a short story called "A Frog's Tale," but I found few people understood what I was getting at. I was reminded of the children in one of the C.S. Lewis, Narnia books who when trying to explain what the Sun was like to the queen of the underworld said it was like a lamp only bigger and brighter. Then in describing Aslan, the lion, they said he was like the queen's cat only bigger and stronger. The queen didn't believe a word they told her, maintaining the children were just saying everything was greater where they came from. How can we describe what others may not have seen?

A friend (Mukesh Bhatt) with whom I shared some of my writings suggested I found some editors. By doing this, as the editors began to understand, I would be able to modify my writings to allow others to understand more easily.

It took a while to find some friends willing to do this but this was the last thing I needed to put this book together. By bouncing my ideas off my unpaid amateur editors I gained a better and better idea, not so much of what I wanted to say, but how it could be said in a way that more people might understand.

As I said in the introduction, in telling my story I hoped to gain a better understanding of myself and to have the reader, say, "Yes, I see what he means." But as well as these obvious objectives I also hope my book will show those considering writing about life that it is not necessarily difficult.

You may ask why did I write the same story three times? I have the following reasons:

1. Part of my target audience is **anyone wanting to start telling others about traumatic events in their lives but not really been able to make a start.** For these people I believe this method of writing a short story first and then building on that works.

2. Many books are discarded after the first page or two have been read. Here I give the reader a good chance of judging the whole book early on. Either they are intrigued or they can stop before starting the main part of the books.

3. The principles I am trying to explain are difficult to explain in words alone, but the use of the fantasy story especially in Version 2 I hope allows the reader to form pictures to relate the ideas to when reading Version 3.

Throughout the book I left out huge chunks of my life as there was no point in putting in anything that did not support the important points I wanted to get across.

Other things happened and new ideas came to me whilst writing. My "miracle cure" is not so simple that it can be explained in 14,000 words. Although memetics is at the core of my staying well, I would some time like to write about my views on other subjects, such as memories and support networks and my own views on self-management.

I know from comments I have already received that memetics can be difficult to grasp. If you are keen to look into this idea then I recommend Dr Susan Blackmore's book on the subject[1].

Here is an extract from that book: "*As I write this book I think of my mind as a battleground of ideas. There are far more of them than can possibly find their way on to the final printed pages. 'I' am not an independent conscious entity creating the ideas from nowhere. Rather, this brain has picked up millions of memes from all its education, reading, and long hours of thinking, and they are all fermenting in there as the fingers type."*

Fortunately for us this process resulted in an amazing book explaining memes far better than I can.

If you have not suffered from mania yourself, you may feel the brief description I gave of one part of one episode was insufficient. To read more detailed descriptions you might contact the Manic Depression Fellowship[2] or visit the Chipmunka Publishing website[3] as they can certainly recommend some good books for this.

Finally if you have managed to read all this I would very much appreciate your comments and if you are inspired (either by me or already inspired) to write about your life I would be interested to hear from you and offer any assistance I can.

Roger Smith, March 2003

I may be contacted at mdflinks@ntlworld.com. Also I hope the website at www.stoppaddling.co.uk will be available at the time this book is published.

[1] *The Meme Machine*, Oxford University Press, ISBN 0 19 850365 2
[2] www.mdf.org.uk, email: mdf@mdf.org.uk, Tel: 020 7793 2600
[3] www.chipmunkapublishing.com

Printed in the United Kingdom by
Lightning Source UK Ltd., Milton Keynes
142408UK00002B/248/A